Wilhelm Heinrich Immanuel Bleek

**Reynard the Fox in South Africa; or, Hottentot Fables and Tales**

Wilhelm Heinrich Immanuel Bleek

**Reynard the Fox in South Africa; or, Hottentot Fables and Tales**

ISBN/EAN: 9783744768689

Printed in Europe, USA, Canada, Australia, Japan

Cover: Foto ©Andreas Hilbeck / pixelio.de

More available books at **www.hansebooks.com**

# REYNARD THE FOX

IN

## SOUTH AFRICA;

OR,

## 𝕳𝖔𝖙𝖙𝖊𝖓𝖙𝖔𝖙 𝕱𝖆𝖇𝖑𝖊𝖘 𝖆𝖓𝖉 𝕿𝖆𝖑𝖊𝖘.

CHIEFLY TRANSLATED FROM ORIGINAL MANUSCRIPTS

IN THE

## LIBRARY

OF

HIS EXCELLENCY SIR GEORGE GREY, K.C.B.

W. H. I. BLEEK, PH.D.

LONDON:

TRÜBNER AND CO., 60, PATERNOSTER ROW.

1864.

# CONTENTS.

—◆—

### I. JACKAL FABLES.

|  |  | PAGE |
|---|---|---|
| 1. | The Lion's Defeat  .  .  . | 1 |
| 2. | The Hunt of the Lion and Jackal  .  . | 3 |
| 3. | The Lion's Share  .  .  .  . | 5 |
| 4. | The Jackal's Bride  .  .  . | 9 |
| 5. | The White Man and the Snake  . | 11 |
| 6. | Another Version of the same Fable  .  . | 13 |
| 7. | Cloud-Eating  .  .  . | 14 |
| 8. | Fish-Stealing  .  . | 16 |
| 9. | Which was the Thief?  .  . | 18 |
| 10. | The Lion's Illness  .  .  . | 19 |
| 11. | The Dove and the Heron  . | 21 |
| 12. | The Cock  .  .  . | 23 |
| 13. | The Leopard and the Ram  . | 24 |

### II. TORTOISE FABLES.

| 14. | The Elephant and the Tortoise  . | 27 |
|---|---|---|
| 15. | The Giraffe and the Tortoise  . | 30 |
| 16. | The Tortoises Hunting the Ostriches  .  . | 32 |

### III. Baboon Fables.

PAGE

17. The Judgment of the Baboon .     33
18. The Lion and the Baboon    .     .     37
19. The Zebra Stallion .     .     .     39
20. The Lost Child (a Tale) .     .     42
21. The Baboon Shepherd (a Tale)     44

### IV. Lion Fables.

22. The Flying Lion     .     .     .    .     45
23. The Lion who thought himself Wiser than his
     Mother .     .     .     .     .     47
24. The Lion who took a Woman's Shape    .    .    50
25. A Woman transformed into a Lion (a Tale)    .    57
26. The Lion and the Bushman (a Tale)     .    .    59

### V. Various Fables.

27. How a Nama Woman outwitted the Elephants .    61
28. A Bad Sister     .     .     .     .    65

### VI. Sun and Moon Fables.

29. Why has the Jackal a long black Stripe on his
     Back ?     .     .     .     .    .    67
30. The Horse cursed by the Sun .     .    .    68
31. The Origin of Death     .     .    .    69
32. Another Version of the same Fable     .    .    71
33. A Third Version of the same Fable     .    .    72

PAGE

34. A Fourth Version of the same Fable . . 73
35. A Zulu Version of the Legend of the "Origin of
Death" . . . . . 74


VII. Heitsi Eibip and other Legends.

36. Heitsi Eibip . . . . 75
37. The Victory of Heitsi Eibip . . . 77
38. Another Version of the same Legend . . 78
39. The Raisin-Eater . . . . 80
40. Origin of the Difference in Modes of Life between
Hottentots and Bushmen . . . 83


VIII. Household Tales.

41. The Little Wise Woman . . . . 85
42. The Unreasonable Child to whom the Dog gave
its Deserts; or, a Receipt for getting any one
to Sleep . . . . . 90

# PREFACE.

My dear Sir George,

In inscribing to you this little book, I do no
more than offer that which is your due, as its appearance is mainly owing to you. It was by your
desire that I wrote, in 1861, to different Missionaries
in South Africa, requesting them to make collections
of Native Literature, similar in nature to those
which, through your instrumentality, had been so
abundantly rescued from oblivion in New Zealand.
I then wrote, among others, to the Rev. G. Krönlein,
Rhenish Missionary at Beerseba, Great Namaqualand; but it was not till after you had left us, on a
new mission of honour and duty, that I received
from him (at five different periods) the original manuscripts from which most of the Fables given here
are translated. He sent us, altogether, twenty-four

Fables, Tales, and Legends, besides twelve Songs of
Praise, thirty-two Proverbs, and twelve Riddles; all
in Hottentot (as taken down by him from the mouth
of the Natives) and German, partly accompanied by
explanatory notes, including fragments of the /Nūsa *
Bushman language.    Mr. Krönlein's manuscripts
fill sixty-five pages, mostly in quarto, with double
columns.

You are aware that the existence of Fables among
the Hottentots was already known to us through Sir
James Alexander's " Expedition of Discovery into
the Interior of Africa " (8vo., two vols., London,
1838), and that some interesting specimens of their
literature had been given by him in that work ; but
that Fables form so extensive a mass of traditionary
Native literature amongst the Namaqua, has first
been brought to light by Mr. Krönlein's communications.    The fact of such a literary capacity existing
among a nation whose mental qualifications it has
been usual to estimate at the lowest standard, is of
the greatest importance ; and that their literary
activity (in contradistinction to the general character

---

* Cisgariepian, from the Nama point of view, *i e.*, to the
North of the Orange River.

of Native literature among Negro nations) has been employed almost in the same direction as that which had been taken by our own earliest literature, is in itself of great significance.

Some questions of no trifling importance and interest are raised by the appearance of such an unlooked-for mine of literary lore, particularly as to the originality of these Fables. Whether they are indeed the real offspring of the desert, and can be considered as truly indigenous Native literature, or whether they have been either purloined from the superior white race, or at least brought into existence by the stimulus which contact with the latter gave to the Native mind (like that resulting in the invention of the Tshiroki and Vei alphabets) may be matters of dispute for some time to come, and it may require as much research as was expended upon the solving of the riddle of the originality of the Ossianic poems.

But whatever may be the ultimate result of such inquiries, whether it will confirm our idea of the originality and antiquity of the main portion of these Hottentot Fables, and consequently stamp them with the character of the oldest and most primitive literary remains of the old mother tongue of the Sexdenoting nations, or whether they have only sprung up recently among the Hottentots from foreign seed—in either case the disposition of the Hottentots to the enjoyment of such Fables, and their easy growth on this arid soil, be it their native or adopted one—shows a much greater congeniality between the Hottentot and European mind than we find between the latter and any of the black races of Africa.

This similarity in the disposition of nations can in itself indeed hardly be considered as a valid proof of common ancestry; but if there be other grounds to make us believe that the nations in question, or at least their languages, are of common origin, it may render us more inclined to assume that such a similarity in their literary taste is derived also from the same source.

The great ethnological difference between the Hottentots and the black nations of South Africa has been a marked fact from almost the earliest acquaintance of Europeans with these parts, and occasional stray guesses (for example, in R. Moffat's " Missionary Labours and Scenes in Southern Africa," 1842, p. 6), have already for some time pointed to a North African origin for the Hottentots.

It is, however, only within the last dozen years

that this has been established as a proved, and, I believe to most observers, an, at first, astonishing fact.
I well remember still the feeling of most curious
interest with which I regarded Knudsen's translation
of Luke's Gospel (vol. i., No. 15 of your Library),
when, in April 1850, it was sent me by the then
Inspector of the Rhenish Mission House, the Rev J.
C. Wallmann, for the purpose of ascertaining whether
the language was in any way akin to those of the
surrounding black nations, and whether, on that account, an already acquired acquaintance with any of
the Hottentot dialects would render it easier for a
Missionary to master one of the Negro or Kafir
tongues.*

---

\* I give here some extracts from Mr. Wallmann's letter,
dated Barmen, 13th April, 1850, which was the only help
of a grammatical or lexical nature then available for me in
my study of this Nama translation of Luke's Gospel :—
"I transmit hereby Luke's Gospel in Namaqua,  . . .
which I can lend you, however, only for four weeks, as I
have already previously promised it to some one else.
"Should your labours permit it, I wish to request you to
make a little trial whether the Namaqua is somewhat
related to the South African family of Languages. For
the present a mere *negative* decision on this point is all
that is wanted, and I should like to have very soon the
opinion of some good philologist regarding it. Moffat

I had, however, at that time not the least idea of
the results to which a knowledge of this language

---

states that when he gave specimens of Namaqua to a
Syrian who came from Egypt, he was told that he (the
Syrian) had seen slaves in the market of Cairo who were of
lighter colour than other Africans, and whose language
resembled that of the Namaqua. Moffat also says that
some ancient authors have mentioned a nation in the
interior of Africa who were very similar to the Hottentots.
Moffat seems himself, however, to ascribe little value to
these accounts, for his guesses fall at once upon the
Chinese. According to communications from our Missionary Knudsen, the Namaqua language seems well
formed. He mentions as personal pronouns :—

| Tita | saaz | χyb | sada | sako | χyku |
|------|------|-----|------|------|------|
| I | thou | he | we | you | they |
| | (*sāts*) | (*//ēip*) | | | (*//ēiku*) |

but to show the modifications which the pronouns undergo
according to the gender, and whether the person (spoken to)
is included or excluded (in the first person plural), the following examples of inclusive or exclusive forms are given :—

"We are captains."

    (incl.) *Sake ke kauauke*  } mascul.
    (excl.) *Sike ke kauauke*  }

    (incl.) *Sase ke kautase*  } fem.
    (excl.) *Sise ke kautase*  }

    (incl.) *Sada ke tana-khoida*  } com.
    (excl.) *Sida ke tana-khoida*  }

    (incl.) *Sakhom ke kauaukhoma*  } dual. mascul.
    (excl.) *Sikhom ke kauaukhoma*  }

would lead me ; and being then mostly occupied with
the study of the Setshuâna and kindred languages—
which seemed to me of paramount interest for com-.
parative philology—I did not at first give undivided
attention to the perusal of this curious volume. I
remarked very soon, however, a striking similarity
between the Hottentot signs of gender and those of
the Coptic language ; but for some time I considered
it as purely accidental, which may be seen from a
letter of mine regarding this subject, published by
Mr. Wallmann, in "Berichten der Rheinischen Mis-

(incl.) *Saam he kautama* ⎱ dual. fem.
(excl.) *Siim ke kautama* ⎰
(incl.) *Saam ke tana-khoima* ⎱ dual. com.
(excl.) *Siim ke tana-khoima* ⎰

"The second person of the plural is said to have not more
than half as many distinctions; and the third person plural
has only the following :—

χ*yku ke kauauga*—mascul.
χ*yte ke kautate*—fem.
χ*yn ke tana-khoina*—com.
χ*ykha ke kauaukha*—dual. mascul.
χ*yra ke kautara*—dual. fem.
χ*yra ke tana-khoira*—dual. com.

"You will therefore oblige me by looking into the
Namaqua Luke, and by having the kindness to write me
your opinion regarding it."

*b*

sions-Gesellschaft" (Reports of the Rhenish Missionary Society, 1850, No. 24, if I am not mistaken in
the number).

Soon, however, what were at first mere isolated
facts, became links, in a chain of evidence, showing
that all those Sexdenoting Languages which were then
known to us in Africa, Asia, and Europe, are members
of one large family, of which the primitive type has,
in most respects, been best preserved to us in the
Hottentot language.

It was even as early as the end of 1850 that I
could write to Mr. Wallmann—"This language (the
Hottentot) is to me at this moment of greater interest
than any other. The facts, of which once before I
have given you some account, have now so increased
upon me, and offer such strong analogies, that there
is no further doubt in my own mind that not only
the Coptic but also the Semitic, and all other languages of Africa (as Berber, the Galla dialect, &c.,
&c.) in which the distinction of the masculine and
feminine gender pervades the whole grammar, are
of common origin."

Part of the result of these researches was then published in my dissertation, "De Nominum Generibus
Linguarum Africæ, Australis, Copticæ, Semiticarum

aliarumque Sexualium" (8vo., Bonn, 6th August, 1851, vol. i., No. 1 of your Library).

I was at that time not aware—nor has it come to my knowledge till within the last few weeks—that on the 10th June, 1851, Dr. J. C. ADAMSON, in communicating to the Syro-Egyptian Society some observations on the analysis of languages, with a special reference to those of South Africa, had stated "That the signs of gender were almost identical in the Namaqua and the Egyptian, and the feminine affix might be considered as being the same in all three" * (Namaqua, Galla, and Old Egyptian).

Another curious agreement on this point, by an apparently independent observer (Mr. J. R. LOGAN), †

---

* Report of the Correspondence and Paper read at the General Meeting of the Syro-Egyptian Society, Session of 1851 and 1852. Read at the Anniversary Meeting, held April 20th, 1852, 8vo. pp. 6, 8.

† "Ethnology of the Indo-Pacific Islands." By J. R. Logan, Esq., Hon. Fellow of the Ethnological Society. Language, Part ii. "The Races and Languages of S.E. Asia, considered in relation to those of the Indo-Pacific Islands," Chapter v., sections i. to vi. [From the Journal of the Indian Archipelago and Eastern Asia, June and December, 1853, to December, 1854.] Singapore: Printed by Jakob Baptist, 8vo., pp. 229, 294, sec. 6. The Semitico-African

was pointed out to me by your Excellency. You also suggested this name of "Sexdenoting Languages." But it is superfluous for me to say any thing of what you have done for the advancement of African, as well as Australian and Polynesian, philology.

It has been justly remarked by our learned friend, Mr. JUSTICE WATERMEYER, that the natural propensities of animals in all parts of the world being so much alike, Fables intended to portray them must also be expected to resemble each other greatly, even to their very details.

But we may well ask why it is that, so far as we know, the Kafir imagination seems not at all inclined to the formation of this class of fictitious tales, though they have otherwise a prolific Native literature of a more or less historic and legendary character. This contrast to what we find among the Hottentots appears not to be accidental, but merely a natural consequence of that difference of structure which distinguishes these two classes of languages, embracing respectively the dialects of the Hottentots on the one

---

Languages, viz.:—1. General Characters, p. 229; 2. Egyptian, p. 248; 3. Hottentot, p. 248; 4. Shemo-Hamitic, or Assyro-Berber, p. 259.

hand, and those of the Kafirs and their kindred nations on the other; in the former (the Hottentot),
as in all other really Sexdenoting Languages, the
grammatical divisions of the nouns into genders, which
do not tally exactly with any distinction observed in
nature, has been brought into a certain reference to
the difference of sex; and on that account this distinction of sex seems in some way to extend even to
inanimate beings, whereby a tendency to the personification of impersonal objects is produced, which
in itself is likely to lead the mind towards ascribing
reason and other human attributes to irrational beings.
This is the real orgin of almost all those poetical
conceptions which we call *Fables* and *Myths*.
Both are based on the personification of impersonal beings—the former by ascribing speech and
reason to the lower animals, whilst the latter sub-
stitute human-like agencies in explanation of celes-
tial and other elementary phenomena in place of
their real cause.

Mythology is, in its origin, most generally either
a mere figure of speech or a poetical explanation
suggested by the grammatical form or etymological
meaning of words, indicating certain striking natural
phenomena. In the primary stage of their produc-

tion, Myths may be supposed to have been always
understood in their true original character; and it
is only when in the course of generations their real
origin has been obscured, and they have become
merely the petrified excrescences of a traditionary
creed, that their apparent absurdity makes them at
first sight almost inexplicable, particularly when
found among nations of a high intelligence.

The humbler sisters of the Myths, the Fables based
on the natural propensities of animals, are not obscured
in their real character so easily as the former, and
have, on that account, more generally retained their
simple usefulness as moral teachers; so, though they
may have preceded even Myths as to the date of their
first conception, they yet outlive them as real and
salutary elements of the best national literatures : not
that Myths had not their own beneficial sphere in the
education of mankind, as leading them on to higher
abstract ideas, and even deeper religious thoughts,
but their very power of exerting a much deeper in-
fluence on the destinies of our race, made it essential
that they should have a more transitory existence in
the civilizing process of the Sexdenoting nations—
who have to give up mythologies so soon as through
them they have gained higher religious ideas—while

Fables, which never claim so high a place among the
elements of furthering the eliminating process of our
species, remain always welcome to most classes of
readers at certain periods of their intellectual deve-
lopment.

Children, and also simple-minded grown-up people,
whose taste has not been spoiled by the poison of
over-exciting reading, will always be amused by the
quaintly expressed moral lessons which they receive
through every good Fable; and the more thorough
student of literature will also regard with pleasure
these first innocent plays of awakening human imagination. To all these the Hottentot Fables offered
here may not be unwelcome as a fresh store of
original compositions, or even as old acquaintances
who gain a new interest in different clothing and
scenery.

To make these Hottentot Fables readable for the
general public, a few slight omissions and alterations
of what would otherwise have been too naked for the
English eye were necessary, but they do not in any
essential way affect the spirit of the Fables. Otherwise, the translation is faithful to the original, though
not exactly literal.

It would of course be presumptuous to believe that

we could here discuss fully the originality or date of composition of these Fables, and all the many questions involved therein.

The modern origin of some of the Fables, as, for instance, that of The Cock (12), Fish-Stealing (8), The Judgment of the Baboon (17), and The Curse of the Horse (30), is very evident; others, *e.g.*, The White Man and the Snake (5 & 6), indicate clearly a European origin. Others, however, have strong claims to be regarded not merely as genuine products of the Hottentot mind, but even as portions of a traditionary Native literature, anterior in its origin to the advent of Europeans.

That the latter is a true view of the subject becomes perhaps the more conclusive by the intimate relations in which, among the Hottentots, Myths still stand to Fables; in fact, a true mythology can hardly be said to exist among them; for Myths (as that of The Origin of Death) are in reality as much Fables as Myths; but we may consider these as analogous to the first germs whence sprung those splendid mythologies which have filled with deep devotional feelings the hearts of many millions among the most intelligent races of the earth.

This higher flight of the imaginative faculty which the Sexdenoting nations possess (through the stimulus of this personification of impersonal things, consequent upon the grammatical structure of their languages), and what it had been to them, becomes the more evident if we compare their literature with that of the Kafirs and other black tribes of South Africa.

As the grammatical structure of languages spoken by the latter does not .in itself suggest personification, these nations are almost, as a matter of course, destitute of Myths as well as Fables. Their literary efforts are, as a general rule, restricted to narrating the doings of men in a more or less historical manner—whence we have a number of household tales, and portions of a fabulous history of these tribes and nations; or their ancestor worship and belief in the supernatural give rise to horrible ghost stories and tales of witchcraft, which would be exciting if they were not generally told in such a long-winded, prosy manner, as must make the best story lose its interest.

Of course for the comparative philologist, and for any one who takes an interest in observing the working of the human mind in its most primitive stages,

*PREFACE.*

these pieces of Kafir and Negro native literature will also have their own interest; it is therefore to be hoped that time and circumstances may soon allow us to publish also the other portions of South African native literature extant in manuscript in your library.

Among these we have principally to mention, as new contributions (received after your departure), twenty-three pieces in o Tyi-hereró, or the Damara language, as written down by natives themselves, copied by the Rev. J. RATH (Rhenish Missionary, formerly in Damara Land, now at Sarepta Knils River), and accompanied with a German translation by him.*

---

* Mr. Rath's Manuscript consists of sixty-one pages, with double columns, foolscap folio. It contains the following pieces :—

1. The Spectre Sweethearts, pp. 1, 2.
2. The Lion Husbands, pp. 2, 5.
3. Tenacity of a Loving Mother's Care, pp. 5, 6.
4. The Girl who ran after her Father's Bird, pp. 6, 12.
5. The Handsome Girl, pp. 12, 15.
6. The Little Bushman Woman, pp. 17, 18.
7. Punishment of Imposition, pp. 19, 21.
8. The Spectre who Fell in Love with his Son's Wife, pp. 22, 23.
9. The Lunatic, p. 23.

Among these pieces there are seven ghost stories, four accounts of transformation of men or animals, eleven other household tales, one legend, and one fable. This last piece (No. 11, pp. 27, 29) is probably of Hottentot origin. I have therefore thought it best to give it a place in this little book (No. 14), where it precedes that Hottentot Fable,to which its conclud-

---

10. The Girls who Escaped from the Hill Damaras, pp. 24, 26.
11. The Elephant and the Tortoise, pp. 27, 29.
12. The Two Wives, pp, 29, 33.
13. The Lion who took different Shapes, pp. 34, 35.
14. The Little Girl left in the Well by her wicked Companions, pp. 35, 38.
15. The Unreasonable Child to whom the Dog gave its Deserts, pp. 39, 43.
16. Rutanga, p. 44.
17. The Ghost of the Man who was Killed by a Rhinoceros in consequence of his Father's Curse, pp. 45, 47.
18. The Trials of Hambeka, a Spirit risen from the Dead, pp. 47, 50.
19. The Little Girl who was teased by an Insect, p. 51.
20. The same as 16 (Rutanga) p. 52.
21. Conjugal Love after Death, p. 53.
22. The Bad Katjungu and the Good Kahavundye, pp. 54, 57.
23. The Wife who went after her Husband, pp. 57, 59.
24. The Little Girl Murdered by the Hill Damara, pp. 59, 61.

ing portions bear such a striking resemblance. It is not unlikely that the beginning of this Hottentot Fable of The Giraffe and the Tortoise is missing. It may have been similar to the beginning of the corresponding one in Damara. As far as it goes the Hottentot Fable is however evidently more original than the o Tyi-hereró text. As a specimen of o Tyi-hereró household tales, I have given Rath's fifteenth piece, the story of The Unreasonable Child to whom the Dog gave its Deserts.

You will also approve of my having added the Zulu legend of the Origin of Death, which in its mixture of Fable and Myth, and even in several details of its composition, shows a great analogy to the Hottentot treatment of the same subject, of which I am able to give here four different versions.

A second version of two or three other fables, and of one legend, has also been given from one of the two important manuscripts in German, regarding the Hottentots and their language, prepared for you by Mr. Knudsen.* The same manu-

---

* The title of Mr. Knudsen's first Manuscript is, "Südafrica: Das Hottentot-Volk; Notizzen (Manuscript) H. C. Knudsen." 4to., p. 12. Its contents are, Bushman Land,

script supplied also a legend of The Origin of Difference in Modes of Life between Hottentots and Bushmen, which we do not yet possess in the Hottentot language.

To make our available stock of Nama Hottentot literature quite complete, three fables and four tales

---

p. 3 ; the different kinds of Rain, p. 3 ; Bethany (in Great Namaqualand), p. 3 ; the Damara, p. 4 ; the Grassy Plain, p. 4 ; the Diseases, pp. 4, 5 ; Birdsnests, p. 5 ; Marriage and Wedding among the Namaqua, p. 5 ; Extent of Authority among the Namaqua, p. 5 ; Similarity with the Jewish manner of Thinking, Counting, Eating, Drinking, Praying, Mode of Speech, and manner of Reckoning Relationship, p. 6 ; Heitsi Eibip or Kabip, p. 7 ; Origin of the Modes of Life of the Namaqua and Bushmen, pp. 7, 8 ; Coming of Age among the Hottentots, p. 8 ; Names of Hottentot Tribes and their probable Etymology, pp. 8, 9 ; Are the Hottentots of Egyptian or Phœnician Origin? p. 9 ; Are the Hottentots of Jewish or Moabitic Origin? pp. 9, 10 ; Appendix, pp. 11, 12.

Mr. Knudsen's second Manuscript has the following title, "Stoff zu einer Grammatik in der Namaquasprache (Manuscript), H. C. Knudsen." 4to. pp. 29. After a few general introductory remarks, and a short explanation of the Hottentot Alphabet, Mr. Knudsen treats of the different Parts of Speech :—I. Nouns, pp. 3, 4 ; II. Adjectives, pp. 4, 5 ; III. Pronouns, pp. 5, 10 ; IV. Numerals, p. 11 ; V. Verbs, pp. 12, 24 ; Interrogative Sentences, pp. 25, 26 ; Concluding Remarks, pp. 26, 29.

have been taken from Sir James Alexander's "Expedition," &c., and inserted here, with only few insignificant verbal alterations.

The "Songs of Praise," given as notes to some of the Fables in this volume, are merely intended as specimens of Hottentot poetry. They can hardly be expected to amuse or interest the general reader—at least, not in the form in which they appear here, though a Longfellow might be able to render some of them in a way that would make them attractive.

In the same manner the materials contained in these Hottentot Fables might be worked out similarly to Goethe's "Reinecke Fuchs;" and we should hereby probably gain an epical composition, which, though not ranking so high as the latter poem, would yet, as regards the interest of its subject-matter, far exceed Longfellow's "Hiawatha" in adaptation to the general taste.

How much Native productions gain when represented skilfully and properly, your admirable work on "Polynesian Mythology" has shown. But you had sterner and more important work on hand, and so I have had to do this without you. That it does not appear in a still more imperfect form, I owe mainly to the help of one who naturally takes the greatest interest in all my pursuits.

In writing the last lines of this Preface, the interest which I feel for these Hottentot Fables is almost fading away before those rich treasures of your library which have just arrived from England ; and as all our present efforts are of course given to the proper settling of these jewels of our library, I can merely send, with grateful acknowledgments, our most fervent wishes for your well-doing, and our sincere hope of seeing you, at no distant day, again in the midst of us.

Believe me,

My dear Sir George,

Yours most faithfully,

W. H. I. BLEEK.

CAPETOWN, *April*, 1863.

# I.

# JACKAL FABLES.

## 1. THE LION'S DEFEAT.

(The original, in the Hottentot language, is in Sir G. Grey's Library, G. Krönlein's Manuscript, pp. 19, 20.)

THE wild animals, it is said, were once assembled at the Lion's. When the Lion was asleep, the Jackal persuaded the little Fox* to twist a rope of ostrich sinews, in order to play the Lion a trick. They took ostrich sinews, twisted them, and fastened the rope to the Lion's tail, and the other end of the rope they tied to a shrub. When the Lion awoke, and saw that he was tied up, he became angry, and called the animals together. When they had assembled, he said (using this form of conjuration)—

* The little Fox, in Nama the *!Kamap*, a small kind of Jackal, who is a swift runner. The Jackal's name is */Girip*. (The / is the dental and the ! the cerebral click ; *vide* Notes to Fables 23 and 27, pp. 47, 62.)

B

" What child of his mother and father's love,
  Whose mother and father's love has tied me ?"

Then answered the animal to whom the question
was first put—

" I, child of my mother and father's love,
  I, mother and father's love, I have not done it."

All answered the same; but when he asked the
little Fox, the little Fox said—

" I, child of my mother and father's love,
  I, mother and father's love, have tied thee !"

Then the Lion tore the rope made of sinews, and
ran after the little Fox.   But the Jackal said—

" My boy, thou son of the lean Mrs. Fox, thou wilt
never be caught."

Truly the Lion was thus beaten in running by the
little Fox.

## 2. THE HUNT OF THE LION AND JACKAL.

(The original, in the Hottentot language, is in Sir G. Grey's
Library, G. Krönlein's Manuscript, pp. 18, 19.)

THE Lion and the Jackal, it is said, were one day
lying in wait for elands. The Lion shot (with the
bow) and missed, but the Jackal hit and sang out,
"Hah! Hah!" The Lion said, "No, you did not
shoot anything. It was I who hit." The Jackal
answered, "Yea, my father, thou hast hit." Then
they went home in order to return when the eland .
was dead, and cut it up. The Jackal, however, turned
back, unknown to the Lion, hit his nose so that the
blood ran on the spoor of the elands, and followed
their track thus, in order to cheat the Lion. When
he had gone some distance, he returned by another
way to the dead eland, and creeping into its carcase,
cut out all the fat.

Meanwhile the Lion followed the bloodstained spoor
of the Jackal, thinking that it was elands' blood, and
only when he had gone some distance did he find out
that he had been deceived. He then returned on the

B 2

Jackal's spoor, and reached the dead eland, where, finding the Jackal in its carcase, he seized him by his tail and drew him out with a swing.

The Lion upbraided the Jackal with these words: "Why do you cheat me?" The Jackal answered: "No, my father, I do not cheat you; you may know it, I think. I prepared this fat for you, father." The Lion said: "Then take the fat and bring it to your mother" (the Lioness); and he gave him the lungs to take to his own wife and children.

When the Jackal arrived, he did not give the fat to the Lion's wife, but to his own wife and children; he gave, however, the lungs to the Lion's wife, and he pelted the Lion's little children with the lungs, saying:

> "You children of the big-pawed one!
> You big-pawed ones!"

He said to the Lioness, "I go to help my father" (the Lion); but he went quite away with his wife and children.

### 3. THE LION'S SHARE.

(From a German original Manuscript in Sir G. Grey's Library, viz., H. C. Knudsen's "Notes on the Hottentots," pp. 11, 12.)

THE Lion and the Jackal went together a-hunting. They shot with arrows. The Lion shot first, but his arrow fell short of its aim; but the Jackal hit the game, and joyfully cried out, "It has hit." The Lion looked at him with his two large eyes; the Jackal, however, did not lose his countenance, but said, "No, Uncle, I mean to say that you have hit." Then they followed the game, and the Jackal passed the arrow of the Lion without drawing the latter's attention to it. When they arrived at a cross-way, the Jackal said, "Dear Uncle, you are old and tired; stay here." The Jackal went then on a wrong track, beat his nose, and, in returning, let the blood drop from it like traces of game. "I could not find anything," he said, "but I met with traces of blood. You had better go yourself to look for it. In the meantime I shall go this other way." The Jackal soon found the killed animal, crept inside of it, and devoured the best portion; but his tail remained outside, and when the Lion arrived, he got hold of it, pulled the Jackal out, and threw him on the ground with these words: "You rascal!" The Jackal rose quickly again, complained of the rough handling, and asked, "What have I then now done, dear Uncle? I was busy cutting out the best part." "Now let us go and fetch our wives," said the Lion; but the Jackal entreated his dear Uncle to remain at the place because he was old. The Jackal went then away, taking with him two portions of the flesh, one for his own wife, but the best part for the wife of the Lion. When the Jackal arrived with the flesh, the children of the Lion saw him, began to jump, and clapping their hands, cried out, "There comes Uncle with flesh!" The Jackal threw, grumbling, the worst portion to them, and said, "There, you brood of the big-eyed one!" Then he went to his own house and told his wife immediately to break up the house, and to go where the killed game was. The Lioness wished to do the same, but he forbade her, and said that the Lion would himself come to fetch her.

When the Jackal, with his wife and children, had arrived in the neighbourhood of the killed animal, he ran into a thorn bush, scratched his face so that it bled, and thus made his appearance before the Lion, to whom he said, "Ah! what a wife you have got. Look here, how she scratched my face when I told her that she should come with us. ·You must fetch her yourself; I cannot bring her." The Lion went home very angry. Then the Jackal said, "Quick, let us build a tower." They heaped stone upon stone, stone upon stone, stone upon stone; and when it was high enough, everything was carried to the top of it. When the Jackal saw the Lion approaching with his wife and children, he cried out to him, "Uncle, whilst you were away we have built a tower, in order to be better able to see game." "All right," said the Lion; "but let me come up to you." "Certainly, dear Uncle; but how will you manage to come up? We must let down a thong for you." The Lion ties himself to the thong, and is drawn up; but when he is nearly at the top the thong is cut by the Jackal, who exclaims, as if frightened, "Oh, how heavy you are, Uncle! Go, wife, fetch me a new thong." ("An old one," he said aside to her.) The Lion is again drawn up, but comes of course down in the same manner. "No," said the Jackal, "that will never do; you must, however, manage to come up high enough, so that you may get a mouthful at least. Then aloud he orders his wife to prepare a good piece, but aside he tells her to make a stone hot, and to cover it with fat. Then he drew up the Lion once more, and, complaining that he is very .heavy to hold, he tells him to open his mouth, whereupon he throws the hot stone down his throat. When the Lion has devoured it, he entreats and requests him to run as quickly as possible to the water.

## 4. THE JACKAL'S BRIDE.

(The original, in the Hottentot language, is in Sir G. Grey's Library, G. Krönlein's Manuscript, pp. 7, 8.)

THE Jackal, it is said, married the Hyena, and carried off a cow belonging to ants, to slaughter her for the wedding; and when he had slaughtered her, he put the cow-skin over his bride; and when he had fixed a pole (on which to hang the flesh), he placed on the top of the pole (which was forked) the hearth for cooking, in order to cook upon it all sorts of delicious food. There came also the Lion to the spot, and wished to go up. The Jackal, therefore, asked his little daughter for a thong with which he could pull the Lion up, and he began to pull him up; and when his face came near to the cooking-pot, he cut the thong in two, so that the Lion tumbled down. Then the Jackal upbraided his little daughter with these words: "Why do you give me such an old thong?" And he added, "Give me a fresh thong." She gave him a new thong, and he pulled the Lion up again, and when his face came near the pot, which stood on the fire, he said, "Open your mouth." Then he put into his mouth a hot piece of quartz which had been boiled together with the fat, and the stone went down, burning his throat. Thus died the Lion.

There came also the ants running after the cow, and when the Jackal saw them he fled. Then they beat the bride in her brookaross dress. The Hyena, believing that it was the Jackal, said—

"You tawny rogue! have you not played at beating
    long enough ?
Have you no more loving game than this ?"

But when she had bitten a hole through the cow-skin, she saw that they were other people; then she fled, falling here and there, yet she made her escape.

## 5. THE WHITE MAN AND THE SNAKE.

(The original, in the Hottentot language, is in Sir G. Grey's
Library, G. Krönlein's Manuscript, pp. 5, 6.)

A WHITE Man, it is said, met a Snake upon whom a
large stone had fallen and covered her, so that she
could not rise. The White Man lifted the stone off
the Snake, but when he had done so, she wanted to
bite him. The White Man said, " Stop ! let us both
go first to some wise people." They went to the
Hyena, and the White Man asked him, " Is it right
that the Snake should want to bite me, though I
helped her, when she lay under a stone and could not
rise ?"

The Hyena (who thought he would get his share of
the White Man's body) said : " If you were bitten
what would it matter ? "

Then the Snake wanted to bite him, but the White
Man said again : " Wait a little, and let us go to
other wise people, that I may hear whether this is
right."

They went and met the Jackal. The White Man
said to the Jackal : " Is it right that the Snake wants

to bite me, though I lifted up the stone which lay upon her?"

The Jackal replied: "I do not believe that the Snake could be covered by a stone and could not rise. Unless I saw it with my two eyes, I would not believe it. Therefore, come let us go and see at the place where you say it happened whether it can be true."

They went, and arrived at the place where it had happened. The Jackal said: "Snake, lie down, and let thyself be covered."

The Snake did so, and the White Man covered her with the stone; but although she exerted herself very much, she could not rise. Then the White Man wanted again to release the Snake, but the Jackal interfered, and said: "Do not lift the stone. She wanted to bite you; therefore she may rise by herself."

Then they both went away and left the Snake under the stone.

## 6. ANOTHER VERSION OF THE SAME FABLE.

(From a German original Manuscript in Sir G. Grey's Library,
H. C. Knudsen's " Notes on the Hottentots," p. 11.)

A Dutchman was walking by himself, and saw a
Snake lying under a large stone. The Snake implored
his help; but when she had become free, she said,
"Now I shall eat you."

The Man answered, " That is not right. Let us
first go to the Hare."

When the Hare had heard the affair, he said, " It
is right." " No," said the Man, " let us ask the
Hyena."

The Hyena declared the same, saying, " It is right."

" Now let us at last ask the Jackal," said the Man
in his despair.

The Jackal answered very slowly and considerately,
doubting the whole affair, and demanding to see first
the place, and whether the Man was able to lift the
stone. The Snake lay down, and the Man, to prove
the truth of his account, put the stone again over her.

When she was fast, the Jackal said, " Now let her
lie there."

## 7. CLOUD-EATING.

(The original, in the Hottentot language, is in Sir G. Grey's Library, G. Krönlein's Manuscript, pp. 30, 31.)

---

### THE HYENA.

Thou who makest thy escape from the tumult!
Thou wide, roomy tree!
Thou who gettest thy share (though with trouble!)
Thou cow who art strained at the hocks! *
Thou who hast a plump round knee!
Thou the nape of whose neck is clothed with hair!
Thou with the skin dripping as if half-tanned!
Thou who hast a round, distended neck!
Thou eater of the Namaqua,
Thou big-toothed one!

---

THE Jackal and the Hyena were together, it is said, when a white cloud rose. The Jackal ascended upon it, and ate of the cloud as if it were fat.

When he wanted to come down, he said to the Hyena, "My sister, as I am going to divide with

---

* "When the Hyena first starts, it appears to be lame on the hind legs, or gone in the loins, as one would say of a horse."—L. LAYARD.

thee, catch me well." So she caught him, and broke his fall. Then she also went up and ate there, high up on the top of the cloud.

When she was satisfied, she said, "My greyish brother, now catch me well." The greyish rogue said to his friend, "My sister, I shall catch thee well. Come therefore down."

He held up his hands, and she came down from the cloud, and when she was near, the Jackal cried out (painfully jumping to one side), "My sister, do not take it ill. Oh me! oh me! A thorn has pricked me, and sticks in me." Thus she fell down from above, and was sadly hurt.

Since that day, it is said, that the Hyena's left hind foot is shorter and smaller than the right one.

## 8. FISH-STEALING.

(From Sir James E. Alexander's " Expedition of Discovery into the Interior of Africa," vol. ii. pp. 246, 247.)

### THE HYENA.

(Addressing her young ones, on her return from a marauding expedition, with regard to the perils she had encountered).

> The fire threatens,
> The stone threatens,
> The assegais threaten,
> The guns threaten,
> Yet you seek food from me.
> My children,
> Do I get anything easily?

ONCE upon a time a Jackal, who lived on the borders of the colony, saw a waggon returning from the sea-side laden with fish. He tried to get into the waggon from behind, but he could not; he then ran on before, and lay in the road as if dead. The waggon came up to him, and the leader cried to the driver, "Here is a fine kaross for your wife!"

" Throw it into the waggon," said the driver, and the Jackal was thrown in.

The waggon travelled on through a moonlight night, and all the while the Jackal was throwing the fish out into the road; he then jumped out himself, and secured a great prize. But a stupid old Hyena coming by, ate more than her share, for which the Jackal owed her a grudge; so he said to her, " You can get plenty of fish, too, if you lie in the way of a waggon as I did, and keep quite still whatever happens."

" So !" mumbled the Hyena.

Accordingly, when the next waggon came from the sea, the Hyena stretched herself out in the road.

" What ugly thing is this ?" cried the leader, and kicked the Hyena. He then took a stick and thrashed her within an inch of her life. The Hyena, according to the directions of the Jackal, lay quiet as long as she could; she then got up and hobbled off to tell her misfortune to the Jackal, who pretended to comfort her.

" What a pity," said the Hyena, " that I have not such a handsome skin as you !"

## 9. WHICH WAS THE THIEF?

(From Sir James E. Alexander's "Expedition of Discovery into the Interior of Africa," vol. ii. p. 250.)

A JACKAL and a Hyena went and hired themselves to a man to be his servants. In the middle of the night the Jackal rose and smeared the Hyena's tail with some fat, and then ate all the rest of it which was in the house. In the morning the man missed his fat, and he immediately accused the Jackal of having eaten it.

"Look at the Hyena's tail," said the rogue, "and you will see who is the thief." The man did so, and then thrashed the Hyena till she was nearly dead.

## 10. THE LION'S ILLNESS.

(The original, in the Hottentot language, is in Sir G. Grey's
Library, G. Krönlein's Manuscript, pp. 29, 30.)

THE Lion, it is said, was ill, and they all went to see
him in his suffering.  But the Jackal did not go,
because the traces of the people who went to see him
did not turn back.  Thereupon, he was accused by
the Hyena, who said, "Though *I* go to look, yet the
Jackal does not want to come and look at the man's
sufferings."

Then the Lion let the Hyena go, in order that she
might catch the Jackal; and she did so, and brought
him.

The Lion asked the Jackal: "Why did you not
come here to see me?"  The Jackal said, "Oh no!
when I heard that my uncle was so very ill, I went
to the witch (doctor), to consult him, whether and
what medicine would be good for my uncle against
the pain.  The doctor said to me, 'Go and tell your
uncle to take hold of the Hyena and draw off her
skin, and put it on while it is still warm.  Then he

c 2

will recover.' The Hyena is one who does not care for my uncle's sufferings."

The Lion followed his advice, got hold of the Hyena, drew the skin over her ears, whilst she howled with all her might, and put it on.

## 11. THE DOVE AND THE HERON.

(The original, in the Hottentot language, is in Sir G. Grey's
Library, G. Krönlein's Manuscript, pp. 13, 14.)

THE Jackal, it is said, came once to the Dove, who
lived on the top of a rock, and said, " Give me one
of your little children." The Dove answered : " I
shall not do anything of the kind." The Jackal said,
"Give it me at once ! Otherwise, I shall fly up to
you." Then she threw one down to him.

He came back another day, and demanded another
little child, and she gave it to him. After the Jackal
had gone, the Heron came, and asked, " Dove, why
do you cry ?" The dove answered him : " The
Jackal has taken away my little children ; it is for this
that I cry." He asked her, " In what manner can
he take them ?" She answered him : " When he
asked me I refused him ; but when he said, ' I shall
at once fly up, therefore give it me,' I threw it down
to him." The Heron said, " Are you such a fool as to
give your children to the Jackals, who cannot fly ?"
Then, with the admonition to give no more, he went
away.

The Jackal came again, and said, " Dove, give me a little child." The Dove refused, and told him that the Heron had told her that he could not fly up. The Jackal said, "I shall catch him."

So when the Heron came to the banks of the water, the Jackal asked him : " Brother Heron, when the wind comes from this side, how will you stand ?" He turned his neck towards him and said, " I stand thus, bending my neck on one side." The Jackal asked him again, " When a storm comes and when it rains, how do you stand ?" He said to him : " I stand thus, indeed, bending my neck down."

Then the Jackal beat him on his neck, and broke his neck in the middle.

Since that day the Heron's neck is bent.

## 12. THE COCK.

(The original, in the Hottentot language, is in Sir G. Grey's Library, G. Krönlein's Manuscript, p. 29.)

THE Cock, it is said, was once overtaken by the Jackal and caught. The Cock said to the Jackal, "Please, pray first (before you kill me) as the white man does." The Jackal asked, "In what manner does he pray? Tell me." "He folds his hands in praying," said the Cock. The Jackal folded his hands and prayed. Then the Cock spoke again: "You ought not to look about you as you do. You had better shut your eyes." He did so; and the Cock flew away, upbraiding at the same time the Jackal with these words: "You rogue! do you also pray?"

There sat the Jackal, speechless, because he had been outdone.

## 13. THE LEOPARD AND THE RAM.

(From Sir James E. Alexander's "Expedition of Discovery into the Interior of Africa," vol. ii. pp. 247, 250.)

A LEOPARD was returning home from hunting on one occasion, when he lighted on the kraal of a Ram. Now the Leopard had never seen a Ram before, and accordingly, approaching submissively, he said, "Good day, friend! what may your name be?"

The other, in his gruff voice, and striking his breast with his forefoot, said, "I am a Ram. Who are you?"

"A Leopard," answered the other, more dead than alive; and then, taking leave of the Ram, he ran home as fast as he could.

A Jackal lived at the same place as the Leopard did, and the latter going to him, said, "Friend Jackal, I am quite out of breath, and am half dead with fright, for I have just seen a terrible-looking fellow, with a large and thick head, and, on my asking him what his name was, he answered roughly, "I am a Ram!"

"What a foolish Leopard you are!" cried the

Jackal, to let such a nice piece of flesh stand! Why did you do so? But we shall go to-morrow and eat it together!"

Next day the two set off for the kraal of the Ram, and as they appeared over a hill, the Ram, who had turned out to look about him, and was calculating where he should that day crop a tender salad, saw them, and he immediately went to his wife, and said, " I fear this is our last day, for the Jackal and Leopard are both coming against us. What shall we do?"

" Don't be afraid," said the wife, " but take up the child in your arms; go out with it, and pinch it to make it cry as if it were hungry." The Ram did so as the confederates came on.

No sooner did the Leopard cast his eyes on the Ram, than fear again took possession of him, and he wished to turn back. The Jackal had provided against this, and made the Leopard fast to himself with a leathern thong, and said, "Come on!" when the Ram cried in a loud voice, and pinching his child at the same time, " You have done well, friend Jackal, to have brought us the Leopard to eat, for you hear how my child is crying for food!"

On hearing these dreadful words, the Leopard, notwithstanding the entreaties of the Jackal to let him loose, set off in the greatest alarm, dragging the

Jackal after him over hill and valley, through bushes
and over rocks, and never stopped to look behind him
till he brought back himself and the half-dead Jackal
to his place again.   And so the Ram escaped.

# II

# TORTOISE FABLES.

---

### THE SPRINGBOK (GAZELLE).

Woe is me! He is one who goes
Where his mother would not let him!
Who rolls off (the rocks),
Rolling himself together like a book.

---

### 14. THE ELEPHANT AND THE TORTOISE.

(The original, in the o Tyi-hereró or Damara language, is in the
Library of Sir G. Grey, J. Rath's Manuscript, pp. 27, 29.)

TWO things, the Elephant and the Rain, had a dispute. The Elephant said, "If you say that you
nourish me, in what way is it that you do so?" The
Rain answered, "If you say that I do not nourish you,
when I go away, will you not die?" And the Rain
then departed.

The Elephant said, "Vulture! cast lots to make

rain for me ?"　The Vulture said, "I will not cast lots."

Then the Elephant said to the Crow, "Cast lots!" who answered, "Give the things with which I may cast lots."　The Crow cast lots and rain fell.　It rained at the lagoons, but they dried up, and only one lagoon remained.

The Elephant went a-hunting.　There was, however, the Tortoise, to whom the Elephant said, "Tortoise, remain at the water!"　Thus the Tortoise was left behind when the Elephant went a-hunting.

There came the Giraffe, and said to the Tortoise, "Give me water!"　The Tortoise answered, "The water belongs to the Elephant."

There came the Zebra, who said to the Tortoise, "Give me water!"　The Tortoise answered, "The water belongs to the Elephant."

There came the Gemsbok, and said to the Tortoise, "Give me water!"　The Tortoise answered, "The water belongs to the Elephant."

There came the Wildebeest, and said, "Give me water!"　The Tortoise said, "The water belongs to the Elephant."

There came the Roodebok, and said to the Tortoise, "Give me water!"　The Tortoise answered, "The water belongs to the Elephant."

There came the Springbok, and said to the Tortoise, "Give me water!" The Tortoise said, "The water belongs to the Elephant."

There came the Jackal, and said to the Tortoise, "Give me water!" The Tortoise said, "The water belongs to the Elephant."

There came the Lion, and said, "Little Tortoise, give me water!" When the little Tortoise was about to say something, the Lion got hold of it and beat it; the Lion drank of the water, and since then the animals drink water.

When the Elephant came back from the hunting, he said, "Little Tortoise, is there water?" The Tortoise answered, "The animals have drunk the water." The Elephant asked, "Little Tortoise, shall I chew you or swallow you down?" The little Tortoise said, "Swallow me, if you please;" and the Elephant swallowed it whole.

After the Elephant had swallowed the little Tortoise, and it had entered his body, it tore off his liver, heart, and kidneys. The Elephant said, "Little Tortoise, you kill me."

So the Elephant died; but the little Tortoise came out of his dead body, and went wherever it liked.

## 15. THE GIRAFFE AND THE TORTOISE.

(The original, in the Hottentot language, is in Sir G. Grey's
Library, G. Krönlein's Manuscript, p. 5.)

---

### THE GIRAFFE.

Thou who descendest river by river,
Thou burnt thornbush ($\neq aro$)!
Thou blue one,*
Who appearest like a distant thornhill
full of people sitting down.

---

THE Giraffe and the Tortoise, they say, met one day.
The Giraffe said to the Tortoise, "At once I could
trample you to death." The Tortoise, being afraid,
remained silent. Then the Giraffe said, "At once I
could swallow you." The Tortoise said, in answer to
this, "Well, I just belong to the family of those whom
it has always been customary to swallow." Then the
Giraffe swallowed the Tortoise; but when the latter
was being gulped down, it stuck in the Giraffe's throat,

* "Because the Giraffe is said to give blue ashes when
burnt."—KRÖNLEIN.

and as the latter could not get it down, he was choked to death.

When the Giraffe was dead, the Tortoise crawled out and went to the Crab (who is considered as the mother of the Tortoise), and told her what had happened.   Then the Crab said—

"The little Crab !   I could sprinkle it under its
      arm with boochoo,*
   The crooked-legged little one, I could sprinkle
      under its arm."

The Tortoise answered its mother and said—

"Have you not always sprinkled me,
   That you want to sprinkle me now ?"

Then they went and fed for a whole year on the remains of the Giraffe.

* In token of approval, according to a Hottentot custom.

## 16. THE TORTOISES HUNTING THE OSTRICHES.

(The original, in the Hottentot language, is in Sir G. Grey's
Library, G. Krönlein's Manuscript, p. 8.)

ONE day, it is said, the Tortoises held a council how they might hunt Ostriches, and they said, "Let us, on both sides, stand in rows near each other, and let one go to hunt the Ostriches, so that they must flee along through the midst of us." They did so, and as they were many, the Ostriches were obliged to run along through the midst of them. During this they did not move, but, remaining always in the same places, called each to the other, "Are you there?" and each one answered, "I am here." The Ostriches hearing this, ran so tremendously that they quite exhausted their strength, and fell down. Then the Tortoises assembled by-and-by at the place where the Ostriches had fallen, and devoured them.

# III.

# BABOON FABLES.

---

Heretse!
Heretse!
Thou thin-armed one,
Who hast thin hands!
Thou smooth bulrush mat,
Thou whose neck is bent.
Thou who art made so as to be lifted up (upon a tree),
Who liftest thyself up.
Thou who wilt not die even behind *that* hill
Which is yet beyond those hills,
That lie on the other side of this far-distant hill.*

---

## 17. THE JUDGMENT OF THE BABOON.

(The original, in the Hottentot language, of this little Namaqualand Fable, is in Sir G. Grey's Library, G. Krönlein's Manuscript,
pp. 33, 35.)

ONE day, it is said, the following story happened.
The Mouse had torn the clothes of Itkler (the tailor),

* With reference to the Baboon's great power of dis-
tancing his pursuers.

D

who then went to the Baboon, and accused the Mouse with these words :—

" In this manner I come to thee :—The Mouse has torn my clothes, but will not know anything of it, and accuses the Cat; the Cat protests likewise her innocence, and says the Dog must have done it; but the Dog denies it also, and declares the Wood has done it; and the Wood throws the blame on the Fire, and says, ' The Fire did it ;' the Fire says, ' *I* have not, the Water did it ;' the Water says, ' The Elephant tore the clothes ;' and the Elephant says, ' The Ant tore them.' Thus a dispute has arisen among them. Therefore I, Itkler, come to thee with this proposition : Assemble the people and try them, in order that I may get satisfaction."

Thus he spake, and the Baboon assembled them for trial. Then they made the same excuses which had been mentioned by Itkler, each one putting the blame upon the other.

So the Baboon did not see any other way of punishing them, save through making them punish each other ; he therefore said—

" Mouse, give Itkler satisfaction."

The Mouse, however, pleaded not guilty. But the Baboon said, " Cat, bite the Mouse." She did so.

He then put the same question to the Cat, and when

she exculpated herself, the Baboon called to the Dog, " Here, bite the Cat."

In this manner the Baboon questioned them all, one after the other, but they each denied the charge. Then he addressed the following words to them, and said—

"Wood, beat the Dog.

Fire, burn the Wood.

Water, quench the Fire.

Elephant, drink the Water.

Ant, bite the Elephant in his most tender parts."

They did so, and since that day they cannot any longer agree with each other.

The Ant enters into the Elephant's most tender parts, and bites him.

The Elephant swallows the Water.

The Water quenches the Fire.

The Fire consumes the Wood.

The Wood beats the Dog.

The Dog bites the Cat.

And the Cat the Mouse.

Through this judgment Itkler got satisfaction, and addressed the Baboon in the following manner:—

"Yes! Now I am content, since I have received satisfaction, and with all my heart I thank thee, Baboon, because thou hast exercised justice on my behalf, and given me redress."

Then the Baboon said, " From to-day I will not any longer be called Jan, but Baboon shall be my name."

Since that time the Baboon walks on all fours, having probably lost the privilege of walking erect through this foolish judgment.(?)

## 18. THE LION AND THE BABOON.

(The original, in the Hottentot language, is in Sir G. Grey's
Library, G. Krönlein's Manuscript, pp. 14, 15.)

### THE BABOON.

Thou hollow-cheeked son
Of a hollow-cheeked one,
My hollow-cheeked one!
Who hast two hip-bones,
High hip-bones,
With which thou sittest on the edge of the rock,
Thou whose face appears like the edge of a rock.

THE Baboon, it is said, once worked bamboos, sitting
on the edge of a precipice, and the Lion stole upon
him. The Baboon, however, had fixed some round,
glistening, eye-like plates on the back of his head.
When, therefore, the Lion crept upon him, he
thought, when the Baboon was looking at him, that
he sat with his back towards him, and crept with all
his might upon him. When, however, the Baboon
turned his back towards him, the Lion thought that
he was seen, and hid himself. Thus, when the

Baboon looked at him, he crept upon him. Whilst the Baboon did this, the Lion came close upon him. When he was near him the Baboon looked up, and the Lion continued to creep upon him. The Baboon said (aside), " Whilst I am looking at him he steals upon me, whilst my hollow eyes are on him."

When at last the Lion sprung at him, he lay (quickly) down upon his face, and the Lion jumped over him, falling down the precipice, and was dashed to pieces.

## 19. THE ZEBRA STALLION.

(The original, in the Hottentot language, is in Sir G. Grey's
Library, G. Krönlein's Manuscript, p. 17.)

———————

### THE ZEBRA.

Thou who art thrown at by the great (shepherd) boys,
Thou whose head the (kirrie's) throw misses!
     Thou dappled fly,
     Thou party-coloured one,
     Who spiest for those,
     That spy for thee!
     Thou who, womanlike,
     Art full of jealousy.

———————

THE Baboons, it is said, used to disturb the Zebra
Mares in drinking. But one of the Mares became
the mother of a foal. The others then helped her
to suckle (the young stallion), that he might soon
grow up.

When he was grown up, and they were in want of
water, they brought him to the water. The Baboons,

seeing this, came, as they formerly were used to do, into their way, and kept them from the water.

While the Mares stood thus, the Stallion stepped forward, and spoke to one of the Baboons, "Thou gum-eater's child!"

The Baboon said to the Stallion, "Please open thy mouth, that I may see what thou livest on." The Stallion opened his mouth, and it was milky.

Then the Stallion said to the Baboon, "Please open thy mouth also, that I may see." The Baboon did so, and there was some gum in it. But the Baboon quickly licked some milk off the Stallion's tongue. The Stallion on this became angry, took the Baboon by his shoulders, and pressed him upon a hot, flat rock. Since that day the Baboon has a bald place on his back.

The Baboon said, lamenting, "I, my mother's child, I, the gum-eater, am outdone by this milk-eater!"

## THE ZEBRA.

Thou //*ari* shrub (*i. e.*, tough shrub, Dutch,
    " critdorn "),
Thou who art of strong smell, ·
Thou who rollest always in soft ground,
Whose body retains the dust,

Thou split kirrie of the shepherd boys,
Thou split knob of a kirrie.
Thou who drivest away by thy neighing
The hunter who seeketh thee.
Thou who crossest all rivers
As if they were but one.

## 20. THE LOST CHILD.—[A Tale.]

(From Sir James E. Alexander's "Expedition of Discovery into
the Interior of Africa," vol. ii. pp. 234, 235.)

THE children belonging to a kraal were playing at
some little distance from the huts with bows and
arrows; in the evening they all returned home, save
one, a boy of five or six years old, who lingered behind, and was soon surrounded by a troop of baboons,
who carried him up a mountain.

The people turned out to recover the boy, and for
days they hunted after him in vain; he was nowhere
to be seen; the baboons also had left the neighbourhood.

A year after this had occurred, a mounted hunter
came to the kraal from a distance, and told the people
that he had crossed at such a place the spoor of
baboons, along with the footmarks of a child. The
people went to the place which the hunter had indi-
cated, and they soon saw what they were in search
of, viz., the boy, sitting on a pinnacle of rock, in company with a large baboon. The moment the people

approached, the baboon took up the boy, and scampered off with him; but, after a close pursuit, the boy was recovered. He seemed quite wild, and tried to run away to the baboons again; however, he was brought back to the kraal, and when he recovered his speech, he said that the baboons had been very kind to him; that they ate scorpions and spiders themselves, but brought him roots, gum, and wild raisins, seeing that he did not touch the two first-named delicacies, and that they always allowed him to drink first at the waters.

## 21. THE BABOON SHEPHERD.—[A Tale.]

(From Sir James E. Alexander's "Expedition of Discovery into the Interior of Africa," vol. ii. pp. 229, 230.)

THE Namaquas say that, not long ago, a man had brought up a young Baboon, and had made it his shepherd. It remained by the flock all day in the field, and at night drove them home to the kraal, riding on the back of one of the goats, which brought up the rear. The Baboon had the milk of one goat allowed to it, and it sucked that one only, and guarded the milk of the others from the children. It also got a little meat from its master. It held the office of shepherd for twelve moons, and then was unfortunately killed in a tree by a Leopard.

# IV.

# LION FABLES.

## 22. THE FLYING LION.

(The original, in the Hottentot language, is in Sir G. Grey's Library, G. Krönlein's Manuscript, pp. 3, 4.)

THE Lion, it is said, used once to fly, and at that time nothing could live before him. As he was unwilling that the bones of what he caught should be broken into pieces, he made a pair of White Crows watch the bones, leaving them behind at the kraal whilst he went a-hunting. But one day the great Frog came there, broke the bones in pieces, and said, "Why can men and animals live no longer?" And he added these words, "When he comes, tell him that I live at yonder pool; if he wishes to see me, he must come there."

The Lion, lying in wait (for game), wanted to fly up, but found he could not fly. Then he got angry, thinking that at the kraal something was wrong, and returned home. When he arrived, he asked, " What have you done that I cannot fly?" Then they answered and said, "Some one came here, broke the bones into pieces, and said, 'If he wants me, he may look for me at yonder pool!'" The Lion went, and arrived while the Frog was sitting at the water's edge, and he tried to creep stealthily upon him. When he was about to get hold of him, the Frog said, "Ho!" and, diving, went to the other side of the pool, and sat there. The Lion pursued him; but as he could not catch him he returned home.

From that day, it is said, the Lion walked on his feet, and also began to creep upon (his game); and the White Crows became entirely dumb since the day that they said, "Nothing can be said of that matter."

## 23. THE LION WHO THOUGHT HIMSELF WISER THAN HIS MOTHER.

(The original, in the Hottentot language, is in Sir G. Grey's Library, G. Krönlein's Manuscript, pp. 31, 33.)

IT is said that when the Lion and /gurikhoisip* (the Only man), together with the Baboon, the Buffalo, and other friends, were playing one day at a certain game, there was a thunderstorm and rain at ǂuro-xaams.† The Lion and /gurikhoisip began to quarrel. "I shall run to the rain-field," said the Lion. /Gurikhoisip said also, " I shall run to the rain-field." As neither would concede this to the other, they separated (angrily). After they had parted, the Lion went to tell his Mother those things which they had both said.

* The / is the dental click, which is " sounded by pressing the tip of the tongue against the front teeth of the upper jaw, and then suddenly and forcibly withdrawing it."— TINDALL.

† The ǂ is the palatal click, described in note to Fable 24, p. 55, and χ is the German ch.

His Mother said to him, " My Father! that Man whose head is in a line with his shoulders and breast, who has pinching weapons, who keeps white dogs, who goes about wearing the tuft of a tiger's tail, beware of him!" The Lion, however, said, "Why need I be on my guard against those whom I know?" The Lioness answered, "My Son, take care of him who has pinching weapons!" But the Lion would not follow his Mother's advice, and the same morning, when it was still pitch dark, he went to ǂ*aroxaams*, and laid himself in ambush. /*Gurikhoisip* went also that morning to the same place. When he had arrived he let his dogs drink, and then bathe. After they had finished they wallowed. Then also the man drank; and, when he had done drinking, the Lion came out of the bush. The dogs surrounded him, as his mother had foretold, and he was speared by /*gurikhoisip*. Just as he became aware that he was speared, the dogs drew him down again. In this manner he grew faint. While he was in this state, /*gurikhoisip* said to the dogs, "Let him alone now, that he may go and be taught by his Mother." So the dogs let him go. They left him, and went home as he lay there. The same night he walked towards home, but whilst he was on the way his strength failed him, and he lamented:

"Mother ! take me up !
Grandmother ! take me up!  Oh me!  Alas !"
At the dawn of day his Mother heard his wailing,
and said—

"My Son, this is the thing which I have told
thee :—

Beware of the one who has pinching weapons,
Who wears a tuft of tiger's tail,
Of him who has white dogs !
Alas !  Thou son of her who is short-eared,
Thou, my short-eared child !
Son of her who eats raw flesh,
Thou flesh-devourer ;
Son of her whose nostrils are red from the
    prey,
Thou with blood-stained nostrils !
Son of her who drinks pit-water,
Thou water-drinker !"

E

## 24. THE LION WHO TOOK A WOMAN'S SHAPE.

(The original, in the Hottentot language, is in Sir G. Grey's Library, G. Krönlein's Manuscript, pp. 60, 65.)

SOME women, it is said, went out to seek roots and herbs and other wild food. On their way home they sat down and said, "Let us taste the food of the field." Now they found that the food picked by one of them was sweet, while that of the others was bitter. The latter said to each other, "Look here! this woman's herbs are sweet." Then they said to the owner of the sweet food, "Throw it away and seek for other"—(sweet-tasted herbs being apparently unpalatable to the Hottentot). So she threw away the food, and went to gather more. When she had collected a sufficient supply, she returned to join the other women, but could not find them. She went therefore down to the river, where the Hare sat lading water, and said to him, "Hare, give me some water that I may drink." But he replied, "This is the cup out of which my uncle (the Lion) and I alone may drink."

She asked again: "Hare, draw water for me that

I may drink." But the Hare made the same reply. Then she snatched the cup from him and drank, but he ran home to tell his uncle of the outrage which had been committed.

The Woman meanwhile replaced the cup and went away. After she had departed the Lion came down, and, seeing her in the distance, pursued her on the road. When she turned round and saw him coming, she sang in the following manner :—

"My mother, she would not let me seek herbs,
    Herbs of the field, food from the field. Hoo!"

When the Lion at last came up with the Woman, they hunted each other round a shrub. She wore many beads and arm-rings, and the Lion said, " Let me put them on!" So she lent them to him, but he afterwards refused to return them to her.

They then hunted each other again round the shrub, till the Lion fell down, and the Woman jumped upon him, and kept him there. The Lion (uttering a form of conjuration) said :

"My Aunt! it is morning, and time to rise;
    Pray, rise from me!"

She then rose from him, and they hunted again after each other round the shrub, till the Woman fell down,

E 2

and the Lion jumped upon her.   She then addressed
him :

> "My Uncle ! it is morning, and time to rise ;
>     Pray, rise from me !"

He rose, of course, and they hunted each other again,
till the Lion fell a second time.   When she jumped
upon him, he said :

> " My Aunt ! it is morning, and time to rise ;
>     Pray, rise from me !"

They rose again and hunted after each other.   The
Woman at last fell down.   But this time, when she
repeated the above conjuration, the Lion said :

> "Hè Kha !   *Is* it morning, and time to rise ?"

He then ate her, taking care, however, to leave her
skin whole, which he put on, together with her dress
and ornaments, so that he looked quite like a woman,
and then went home to her kraal.

When this counterfeit woman arrived, her little
sister, crying, said, " My sister, pour some milk out
for me."   She answered, " I shall not pour you out
any."   Then the child addressed their Mother :
" Mama, do pour out some for me."   The Mother of
the kraal said, " Go to your sister, and let her give

it to you!" The little child said again to her sister, "Please, pour out for me!" She, however, repeated her refusal, saying, "I will not do it." Then the Mother of the kraal said to the little one, "I refused to let her (the elder sister) seek herbs in the field, and I do not know what may have happened; go therefore to the Hare, and ask him to pour out for you."

So the Hare gave her some milk; but her elder sister said, "Come and share it with me." The little child then went to her sister with her bamboo (cup), and they both sucked the milk out of it. Whilst they were doing this, some milk was spilt on the little one's hand, and the elder sister licked it up with her tongue, the roughness of which drew blood; this, too, the Woman licked up.

The little child complained to her Mother: "Mama, sister pricks holes in me, and sucks the blood." The Mother said, "With what lion's nature your sister went the way that I forbade her, and returned, I do not know."

Now the cows arrived, and the elder sister cleansed the pails in order to milk them. But when she approached the cows with a thong (in order to tie their fore-legs), they all refused to be milked by her.

The Hare said, "Why do not you stand before the cow?" She replied, "Hare, call your brother, and do you two stand before the cow." Her husband said, " What has come over her that the cows refuse her ? These are the same cows she always milks." The Mother (of the kraal) said, " What has happened this evening ? These are cows which she always milks without assistance. What can have affected her that she comes home as a woman with a lion's nature ?"

The elder daughter then said to her Mother, " I shall not milk the cows." With these words she sat down. The Mother said therefore to the Hare, " Bring me the bamboos, that I may milk. I do not know what has come over the girl."

So the Mother herself milked the cows, and when she had done so, the Hare brought the bamboos to the young wife's house, where her husband was, but she (the wife) did not give him (her husband) anything to eat. But when at night time she fell asleep, they saw some of the Lion's hair, which was hanging out where he had slipped on the woman's skin, and they cried, " Verily ! this is quite another being. It is for this reason that the cows refused to be milked."

Then the people of the kraal began to break up the hut in which the Lion lay asleep. When they took off the mats, they said (conjuring them), " If thou art favourably inclined to me, O mat, give the sound ' *sawa* ' " (meaning, making no noise).

To the poles (on which the hut rested) they said, "If thou art favourably inclined to me, O pole, thou must give the sound ǂ*gara.*"*

They addressed also the bamboos and the bed-skins in a similar manner.

Thus gradually and noiselessly they removed the hut and all its contents. Then they took bunches of grass, put them over the Lion, and lighting them, said, "If thou art favourably inclined to me, O fire, thou must flare up, '*boo boo,*' before thou comest to the heart."

So the fire flared up when it came towards the heart, and the heart of the Woman jumped upon the ground. The Mother (of the kraal) picked it up, and put it into a calabash.

The Lion, from his place in the fire, said to the Mother (of the kraal), "How nicely I have eaten your daughter." The Woman answered, "You have also now a comfortable place!"  *  *  *

Now the Woman took the first milk of as many cows as calved, and put it into the calabash where her daughter's heart was; the calabash increased in size, and in proportion to this the girl grew again inside it.

---

* ǂ Indicates the palatal click, which is sounded by pressing the tip of the tongue, with as flat a surface as possible, against the termination of the palate at the gums, and withdrawing it suddenly and forcibly.

One day, when the Mother (of the kraal) went out to fetch wood, she said to the Hare, "By the time that I come back you must have everything nice and clean." But during her Mother's absence, the girl crept out of the calabash, and put the hut in good order, as she had been used to do in former days, and said to the Hare, "When mother comes back and asks, ' Who has done these things?' you must say, ' I, the Hare, did them.'" After she had done all, she hid herself on the stage.*

When the Mother (of the kraal) came home, she said, "Hare, who has done these things? They look just as they used when my daughter did them." The Hare said, "I did the things." But the Mother would not believe it, and looked at the calabash. Seeing it was empty, she searched the stage and found her daughter. Then she embraced and kissed her, and from that day the girl stayed with her mother, and did everything as she was wont in former times ; but she now remained unmarried.

---

* The stage is that apparatus in the background of the hut (built of mats) opposite the door, upon which the Hottentots hang their bamboos, bags of skins, and other things, and under which the women generally keep their mats.

## 25. A WOMAN TRANSFORMED INTO A LION.
### [A TALE.]

(From Sir James E. Alexander's "Expedition of Discovery into
the Interior of Africa," vol. ii. pp. 197, 198.)

ONCE upon a time a certain Hottentot was travelling
in company with a Bushwoman, carrying a child on
her back. They had proceeded some distance on their
journey, when a troop of wild horses appeared, and the
Man said to the Woman, "I am hungry; and as I
know you can turn yourself into a Lion, do so now,
and catch us a wild horse, that we may eat."

The Woman answered, " You will be afraid."

"No, no," said the Man; " I am afraid of dying of
hunger, but not of you."

Whilst he was yet speaking, hair began to appear
at the back of the Woman's neck; her nails gradually
assumed the appearance of claws, and her features
altered. She sat down the child.

The Man, alarmed at the change, climbed a tree
close by. The Woman glared at him fearfully, and
going to one side, she threw off her skin petticoat, when

a perfect Lion rushed into the plain. It bounded and crept among the bushes towards the wild horses, and springing on one of them, it fell, and the Lion lapped its blood. The Lion then came back to where the child was crying, and the man called from the tree, "Enough, enough! don't hurt me. Put off your lion's shape, I'll never ask to see this again."

The Lion looked at him and growled. "I'll remain here till I die," said the Man, "if you don't become a woman again." The mane and tail then began to disappear, the Lion went towards the bush where the skin petticoat lay; it was slipped on, and the woman, in her proper shape, took up the child. The Man descended and partook of the horse's flesh, but never again asked the Woman to catch game for him.

## 26. THE LION AND THE BUSHMAN.

### [A TALE.]

(From Sir James E. Alexander's "Expedition of Discovery into the Interior of Africa," vol. ii. p. 51.)

A BUSHMAN was, on one occasion, following a troop of zebras, and had just succeeded in wounding one with his arrows, when a Lion sprang out from a thicket opposite, and showed every inclination to dispute the prize with him. The Bushman being near a convenient tree, threw down his arms, and climbed for safety to an upper branch. The Lion, allowing the wounded zebra to pass on, now turned his whole attention towards the Bushman, and walking round and round the tree, he ever and anon growled and looked up at him. At length the Lion lay down at the foot of the tree, and kept watch all night. Towards morning sleep overcame the hitherto wakeful Bushman, and he dreamt that he had fallen into the Lion's mouth. Starting from the effects of his dream, he lost his hold, and, falling from the branch, he alighted heavily on the Lion; on which the monster, thus unexpectedly saluted, ran off with a loud roar, and the Bushman, also taking to his heels in a different direction, escaped in safety.

# V.

# VARIOUS FABLES.

---

### THE ELEPHANT.

Thou tall acacia full of branches,
Thou ebony tree with leaves spread round about.

---

## 27. HOW A NAMA WOMAN OUTWITTED THE ELEPHANTS.

(The original, in the Hottentot language, is in Sir G. Grey's
Library, G. Krönlein's Manuscript, pp. 1, 3.)

AN Elephant, it is said, was married to a Nama Hottentot woman, whose two brothers came to her secretly, because they were afraid of her husband. Then she went out as if to fetch wood, and putting them within the wood, she laid them on the stage.* Then she said, "Since I married into this kraal, has a wether been slaughtered also for me?" And her blind mother-

---

* *Vide* Note to Fable 24, p. 56.

in-law answered, "Umph! things are said by the wife of my eldest son, which she never said before."

Thereupon the Elephant, who had been in the field, arrived, and smelling something, rubbed against the house. "Ha," said his wife, "what I should not have done formerly, I do now. On what day did you slaughter a wether for me?" Then the mother-in-law said to him : "As she says things which she did not say (before), do it now."

In this manner a wether was slaughtered (for her), which she roasted whole, and then, in the same night (after supper), asked her mother-in-law the following questions :—"How do you breathe when you sleep the sleep of life? (light sleep, half-conscious.) And how when you sleep the sleep of death?" (deep sleep.)

Then the mother-in-law said, "Umph, an evening full of conversation! When we sleep the sleep of death, we breathe thus : ' *sūi sūi !*' and when we sleep the sleep of life we breathe thus : ' *Xou !áwaba ! Xou !áwaba!*' " *

Thus the wife made everything right whilst they fell asleep. Then she listened to their snoring, and

---

* *X* is the German *ch*, and *!* the cerebral click of the Hottentot language, which is " sounded by sending up the tip of the tongue against the roof of the palate, and withdrawing it forcibly and suddenly."—TINDALL.

when they slept thus, *sūi sūi*, she rose and said to her
two brothers, "The sleep of death is over them, let
us make ready." They rose and went out, and she
broke up the hut* (to carry away all that she could),
and took the necessary things, and said, "That thing
which makes any noise wills my death." So they
kept altogether quiet.

When her two brothers had packed up, she went
with them between the cattle, but she left at home
one·cow, one ewe, and one goat, and directed them,
saying to the cow, "You must not low as if you were
by yourself alone, if you do not wish for my death;"
and she taught the ewe and the goat the same.

Then they departed with all the other cattle, and
those who were left behind lowed during the night as
if they were many, and as they lowed as if they were
still all there, the Elephant thought, "They are all
there." But when he rose in the morning, he saw
that his wife and all the cattle were gone. Taking
his stick into his hands, he said to his mother, "If I
fall the earth will tremble." With these words he
followed them. When they saw him approaching,
they ran fast to the side, against a piece of rock (at a

* Hottentot huts being merely made of skins stretched
over a frame, are carried about by the people in their
wanderings.

narrow spot), and she said, "We are people, behind whom a large (travelling) party comes. Stone of my ancestors! divide thyself for us." Then the rock divided itself, and when they had passed through it, it closed again (behind them).

Then came the Elephant, and said to the rock, "Stone of my ancestors! divide thyself also for me." The rock divided itself again, but when he had entered, it closed upon him. Thus died the Elephant, and the earth trembled. The mother at her hut said then, "As my eldest son said, it has happened. The earth shakes."

## 28. A BAD SISTER.

(The original, in the Hottentot language, is in Sir G. Grey's
Library, G. Krönlein's Manuscript, pp. 15, 16.)

COPPER and Weather, it is said, were man and wife,
and begat a daughter, who married amongst other
people.

Her three brothers came to visit her; and she did
not know them (as such), though the people said, "Do
not you see they are your brothers?" She deter-
mined to kill them at night. They had, however, a
Guinea-fowl to watch them.

When the Copper-Weather relative crept near, in
order to kill the men, the Guinea-fowl made a noise
to put them on their guard. They were thus warned
of the danger; but afterwards they fell asleep again.
Then she stole again upon them. The Guinea-fowl
made a noise, but broke the rope by which it had
been fastened, and ran home. She then killed her
brothers. When the Guinea-fowl came near home
it wept :—

F

" The Copper-Weather relative has killed her
    brothers !

Alas ! she has killed her brothers !"

The wife heard it, and said to her husband—

" Do not you hear what the bird weeps for ?
    You who sit here upon the ground working
    bamboos."

The man said, " Come and turn yourself into a
mighty thunderstorm, and I will be a strong wind."
So they transformed themselves accordingly, and
when they came near to the kraal (where their sons
had been killed), they combined and became a fire,
and as a fiery rain they burnt the kraal and all its
inhabitants.

# VI.

# SUN AND MOON FABLES.

## 29. WHY HAS THE JACKAL A LONG BLACK STRIPE ON HIS BACK?

*(The original, in the Hottentot language, is in Sir G. Grey's Library, G. Krönlein's Manuscript, p. 16.)*

THE Sun, it is said, was one day on earth, and the men who were travelling saw him sitting by the wayside, but passed him without notice. The Jackal, however, who came after them, and saw him also sitting, went to him and said, "Such a fine little child is left behind by the men." He then took the Sun up, and put it into his awa-skin (on his back). When it burnt him, he said, "Get down," and shook himself; but the Sun stuck fast to his back, and burnt the Jackal's back black from that day.

F 2

## 30. THE HORSE CURSED BY THE SUN.

(The original, in the Hottentot language, of this little Namaqualand Fable, is in Sir G. Grey's Library, G. Krönlein's
   Manuscript, p. 53.)

IT is said that once the Sun was on earth, and caught
the Horse to ride it. But it was unable to bear his
weight, and therefore the Ox took the place of the
Horse, and carried the Sun on its back. Since that
time the Horse is cursed in these words, because it
could not carry the Sun's weight:—

" From to-day thou shalt have a (certain) time of
      dying.
This is thy curse, that thou hast a (certain) time of
      dying.
And day and night shalt thou eat,
But the desire of thy heart shall not be at rest,
Though thou grazest till morning and again until
      sunset.
Behold, this is the judgment which I pass upon thee,"
      said the Sun.

   Since that day the Horse's (certain) time of dying
commenced.

## 31. THE ORIGIN OF DEATH.

(The original, in the Hottentot language, is in Sir G. Grey's Library, G. Krönlein's Manuscript, pp. 33, 34.)

THE Moon, it is said, sent once an Insect to Men, saying, "Go thou to Men, and tell them, 'As I die, and dying live, so ye shall also die, and dying live.'" The Insect started with the message, but whilst on his way was overtaken by the Hare, who asked: "On what errand art thou bound?" The Insect answered: "I am sent by the Moon to Men, to tell them that as she dies, and dying lives, they also shall die, and dying live." The Hare said, "As thou art an awkward runner, let me go" (to take the message). With these words he ran off, and when he reached Men, he said, "I am sent by the Moon to tell you, 'As I die, and dying perish, in the same manner ye shall also die and come wholly to an end.'" Then the Hare returned to the Moon, and told her what he had said to Men. The Moon reproached him angrily, saying, "Darest thou tell the people a thing which I have not said?" With these words she took up a piece of wood, and struck him on the nose. Since that day the Hare's nose is slit.

## 32. ANOTHER VERSION OF THE SAME FABLE.

(From H. C. Knudsen's "Gross-Namaqualand," 12mo., Barmen, 1848, pp. 27, 28.)

THE Moon dies, and rises to life again.  The Moon said to the Hare, "Go thou to Men, and tell them, ' Like as I die and rise to life again, so you also shall die and rise to life again.' "  The Hare went to the Men, and said, " Like as I die and do not rise to life again, so you shall also die, and not rise to life again.' When he returned, the Moon asked him, "What hast thou said?"  " I have told them, ' Like as I die and do not rise to life again, so you shall also die and not rise to life again.' "  "What," said the Moon, "hast thou said that?"  And she took a stick and beat the Hare on his mouth, which was slit by the blow.  The Hare fled, and is still fleeing."*

---

* "We are now angry with the Hare," say the old Namaqua, "because he brought such a bad message, and therefore we dislike to eat his flesh."—KNUDSEN.

## 33. A THIRD VERSION OF THE SAME FABLE.

(From an original Manuscript in English, by Mr. John Priestley, in Sir G. Grey's Library.)

THE Moon, on one occasion, sent the Hare to the earth to inform Men that as she (the Moon) died away and rose again, so mankind should die and rise again. Instead, however, of delivering this message as given, the Hare, either out of forgetfulness or malice, told mankind that as the Moon rose and died away, so Man should die and rise no more. The Hare, having returned to the Moon, was questioned as to the message delivered, and the Moon, having heard the true state of the case, became so enraged with him that she took up a hatchet to split his head; falling short, however, of that, the hatchet fell upon the upper lip of the Hare, and cut it severely. Hence it is that we see the "Hare-lip." The Hare, being duly incensed at having received such treatment, raised his claws, and scratched the Moon's face; and the dark parts which we now see on the surface of the Moon are the scars which she received on that occasion.

## 34. A FOURTH VERSION OF THE SAME FABLE.

(From Sir James E. Alexander's "Expedition of Discovery into the Interior of Africa," vol. i. p. 169.)

THE Moon, they say, wished to send a message to Men, and the Hare said that he would take it. "Run, then," said the Moon, "and tell Men that as I die and am renewed, so shall they also be renewed." But the Hare deceived Men, and said, "As I die and perish, so shall you also."*

* Old Namaquas will not therefore touch Hare's flesh; but the young men may partake of it; that is, before the ceremony of making them men is performed, which merely consists in slaughtering and eating an ox or a couple of sheep.—ALEXANDER.

## 35. A ZULU VERSION OF THE LEGEND OF THE "ORIGIN OF DEATH."

(From Manuscript, "Zulu Legends," No. 214 of Sir G. Grey's Library, vol. i. part i. p. 107.)

GOD (*Unknlunkuln*) arose from beneath (the seat of the spiritual world, according to the Zulu idea), and created in the beginning\* men, animals, and all things. He then sent for the Chameleon, and said, " Go, Chameleon, and tell Men that they shall not die." The Chameleon went, but it walked slowly, and loitered on the way, eating of a shrub called *Bukwebezane*.

When it had been away some time, God sent the Salamander after it, ordering him to make haste and tell Men that they should die. The Salamander went on his way with this message, outran the Chameleon, and, arriving first where the Men were, told them that they must die.

\* *Ohlangeni*. *Vide* Colenso's " Zulu-English Dictionary," p. 179.

# VII

# HEITSI EIBIP

## AND OTHER LEGENDS.

### 36. HEITSI EIBIP.

(From a German original Manuscript in Sir G. Grey's Library,
H. C. Knudsen's " Notes on the Hottentots," p. 7.)

HEITSI EIBIP, or *Kabip*, was a great and celebrated
sorcerer among the Namaqua. He could tell secret
things, and prophesy what was to happen afterwards.

Once he was travelling with a great number of
people, and an enemy pursued them. On arriving
at some water he said, "My grandfather's father,
open thyself that I may pass through, and close thyself afterwards." So it took place as he had said, and
they went safely through. Then their enemies tried
to pass through the opening also, but when they were
in the midst óf it, it closed again upon them, and they
perished.*

* Knudsen, who heard this legend from the Hottentot
Petrus Friedrik, was afterwards informed that *Heitsi Eibip*

*Heitsi Kabip* died several times, and came to life again. When the Hottentots pass one of his graves they throw a stone on it for good luck.*

*Heitsi Eibip* could take many different forms. Sometimes he appeared handsome, very handsome, or his hair grew long down to his shoulders; at other times it was again short.

---

was not the person meant in this tale. It looks very much like the end of our 27th Fable, of the Woman who outwitted the Elephants.

* Sir James E. Alexander, in his "Expedition of Discovery into the Interior of Africa," vol. i. p. 166, speaking of the people at Warm Bath, or Nisbett Bath, says:—"These Namaquas thought that they came from the East. In the country there is occasionally found (besides the common graves covered with a heap of stones) large heaps of stones, on which had been thrown a few bushes; and if the Namaquas are asked what these are, they say that *Heije Eibib,* their Great Father, is below the heap; they do not know what he is like, or what he does; they only imagine that he also came from the East, and had plenty of sheep and goats; and when they add a stone or branch to the heap, they mutter, 'Give us plenty of cattle.'"

## 37. THE VICTORY OF HEITSI EIBIP.

(From a German original Manuscript in Sir G. Grey's Library,
H. C. Knudsen's " Notes on the Hottentots," p. 7.)

AT first they were two. One had made a large hole
in the ground, and sat by it, and told passers-by to
throw a stone at his forehead. The stone, however,
rebounded and killed the person who had thrown it,
so that he fell into the hole. At last *Heitsi Eibip*
was told that in this manner many people died. So
he arose and went to the man, who challenged *Heitsi
Eibip* to throw (a stone) at him. The latter, however,
declined, for he was too prudent ; but he drew the
man's attention to something on one side, and while
he turned round to look at it, *Heitsi Eibip* hit him
behind the ear, so that he died and fell into his own
hole. After that there was peace, and people lived
happily.*

\* Sir James Alexander, in his " Expedition of Discovery
into the Interior of Africa," vol. ii. p. 250, states :—" On
the 3rd of August the waggon went on to Aneip, or Wet
Foot, and I went out of the way with Jan Buys, and two or
three men, to see a hole, which was supposed to be inhabited
by *Heije Eibib*, and was the wonder of the country."

## 38. ANOTHER VERSION OF THE SAME LEGEND.

(The original, in the Hottentot language, is in Sir G. Grey's Library, G. Krönlein's Manuscript, p. 36.)

ALL men who came near to that hole were, it is said, pushed down into it by the ǂ*Gā* ǂ*gorip*\* (the pusher into the hole), as he knew well where it lay. Whilst he was thus employed, there came the *Heitsi Eibip*, called also *Heigeip*, and saw how the ǂ*Gā* ǂ*gorip* treated the people.

Then these two began to hunt each other round the hole, saying—

" Push the *Heigeip* down !"

" Push the ǂ*Gā* ǂ*gorip* down !"

"Push the *Heigeip* down !"

" Push the ǂ*Gā* ǂ*gorip* down !"

With these words they hunted each other round for some time; but at last the *Heigeip* was pushed

\* The ǂ is the palatal click, described in Note to Fable 24, p. 55; and indicates the nasal pronunciation of a syllable.

down. Then he said to the hole, "Support me a little," and it did. Thus, being supported, he came out; and they hunted each other again with the same words :—

> "Push the *Heigeip* down !"
> "Push the ǂ*Gā* ǂ*gorip* down !"

A second time the *Heigeip* was pushed down, and he spoke the same words : "Support me a little," and thus got out again.

Once more these two hunted after each other, till at last the ǂ*Gā* ǂ*gorip* was pushed down, and *he* came not up again. Since that day men breathed freely and had rest from their enemy, because he was vanquished.

## 39. THE RAISIN-EATER.

(The original, in the Hottentot language, is in Sir G. Grey's Library, G. Krönlein's Manuscript, pp. 34, 35.)

IT is said that when *Heitsi Eibip* was travelling about with his family, they came to a valley in which the raisin-tree was ripe, and he was there attacked by a severe illness. Then his young (second) wife said, "This brave one is taken ill on account of these raisins; death is here at the place." The old man (*Heitsi Eibip*), however, told his son *! Urisip* \* (the whitish one), "I shall not live, I feel it; thou must, therefore, cover me when I am dead with soft stones." And he spoke further, "This is the thing which I order you to do:—'Of the raisin-trees of this valley ye shall not eat. For if ye eat of them I shall infect you, and ye will surely die in a similar way.'"

His young wife said, "He is taken ill on account of the raisins of this valley. Let us bury him quickly, and let us go."

\* The *!* is the cerebral click described in Note to Fable 27, p. 62.

So he died there, and was covered flatly with soft stones according as he had commanded. Then they went away from him.

When they had moved to another place, and were unpacking there, they heard always from the side whence they came a noise as of people eating raisins and singing. In this manner the eating and singing ran :—

> " I, father of *!Urisip*,
> Father of this unclean one,
> I, who had to eat these raisins, and died,
> And dying live."

The young wife perceived that the noise came from the side where the old man's grave was, and said, " *!Urisip!* Go and look!" Then the son went to the old man's grave, where he saw traces which he recognised to be his father's footmarks, and returned home. Then the young wife said, " It is he alone ; therefore act thus :—

> " Do so to the man who ate raisins on the windward
>> side,
> Take care of the wind that thou creepest upon him
>> from the leeward ;
> Then intercept him on his way to the grave,

G

And when thou hast caught him, do not let him go."

He did accordingly, and they came between the grave and *Heitsi Eibip* who, when he saw this, jumped down from the raisin-trees, and ran quickly, but was caught at the grave. Then he said :

"Let me go ! For I am a man who has been dead that I may not infect you !" But the young wife said, " Keep hold of the rogue !" So they brought him home, and from that day he was fresh and hale.

## 40. ORIGIN OF THE DIFFERENCE IN MODES OF LIFE BETWEEN HOTTEN-TOTS AND BUSHMEN.

(From a German original Manuscript in Sir G. Grey's Library, H. C. Knudson's "Notes on the Hottentots," pp. 7, 8.)

IN the beginning there were two. One was blind, the other was always hunting. This hunter found at last a hole in the earth, from which game proceeded, and killed the young. The blind man, feeling and smelling them, said, "They are not game, but cattle."

The blind man afterwards recovered his sight, and going with the hunter to this hole, saw that they were cows with their calves. He then quickly built a kraal (fence made of thorns) round them, and anointed himself, just as Hottentots (in their native state) are still wont to do.

When the other, who now with great trouble had to seek his game, came and saw this, he wanted to anoint himself also. " Look here !" said the other, " you must throw the ointment into the fire, and after-wards use it." He followed this advice, and the flames flaring up into his face, burnt him most miserably ; so that he was glad to make his escape. The other, however, called to him : " Here, take the kirri (a knobstick), and run to the hills, to hunt there for honey."

Hence sprung the race of Bushmen.

# VIII

# HOUSEHOLD TALES.

## 41. THE LITTLE WISE WOMAN.

(The original, in the Hottentot language, is in Sir G. Grey's
Library, G. Krönlein's Manuscript, p. 53.)

A GIRL, it is said, went to seek for onions. As she
arrived at the place where they grew, she met with
some men, one of whom was blind (*i.e.*, half-blind,
having only one eye). As she dug (for the onions)
the men helped her, digging also. When her sack
was full, they said to her, " Go, tell the other girls,
that many of you may come." So she went home and
told her companions, and early the next morning they
started. But a little girl followed them. The other
girls said, "Let the little girl go back." But her elder
sister protested against this, saying, " She runs by
herself, you need not put her into your awa-skin."

So they went all together, and having reached the
onion-ground, began to dig. Now the little girl saw

traces of feet, and said to the one who had guided them thither, "Wonderful! whence so many traces? Were you not alone here?" The other replied, "I walked about and looked out; therefore they must of course be many." The child, however, did not believe that if the other girl had been alone the traces could be many, and felt uneasy; for she was a wise little woman. From time to time she rose (from her work) and peeped about, and once, while doing this, found by chance an ant-eater's hole. Still further spying about, she perceived some men, but they did not see her. She then returned and continued digging with the other girls, without, however, saying anything. But in the midst of their work she always rose and looked about her. So the others asked her, "Why do you always spy about you, and leave off digging? What a girl!" But she continued her work in silence. When she rose from it again, she saw the men approaching. As they drew near the One-eyed blew through a reed pipe the following air:—

"To-day there shall blood flow, blood flow, blood flow!"

The little girl understood what was blown on the reed. She said to the elder ones, whilst they were dancing, "Do you also understand the tune that is blown on the reed?" But they only said, "What a child she is !" So she mixed in the dance with the others; but managed while so doing to tie her sister's caross-cloak to her own, and in this manner they danced on, till it became very noisy, and then they found an opportunity to slip away.

On their way out the little sister asked, " Do you understand the reed—I mean what is blown on it ?" She answered, "I do not understand it." Then the little girl explained to her that the tune on the reed said, " To-day blood shall flow !" When they walked along, the little girl let her elder sister go first, and herself followed, walking backwards, and carefully stepping in her sister's traces, so that they thus left only one set of footmarks, and these going in a contrary direction. In this manner they arrived at the ant-eater's hole.

But the men killed all those girls who had remained dancing with them. When the eldest of those who had escaped heard their wailing, she said, " Alas, my sisters !" But the younger one answered her, " Do you think you would have lived if you had remained there ?"

Now "One-eye" was the first to miss the sisters, and said to the other men, " Where may the two handsome girls be who danced with me ?" The others replied, " He lies. He has seen with his eye (satirically meaning he had seen wrongly). But "One-eye" insisted that " two girls were truly missing." Then they went to find their spoor, but the traces had been rendered indistinct enough to puzzle them.

When the men arrived at the ant-eater's hole, they could not see that the footmarks went further, so they spied into the hole, but saw nothing. Then " One-eye " looked also, and he saw the girls, and cried, " There they sit." The others now looked again, but still saw nothing; for the girls had covered themselves with cobwebs.

One of the men then took an assegai, and piercing through the upper part of the hole, hit the heel of the larger girl. But the little wise woman took hold of the assegai, and wiped off the blood. The elder sister was about to cry, but the little one warned her not.

When " One-eye " spied again, the little girl made big eyes at him. He said, " There she sits." The others looked too, but as they could see nothing they said (satirically), " He has only seen with his eye."

At last the men got thirsty, and said to " One-eye," " Stay you here, and let us go to drink, and when we have returned you may go also."

When " One-eye" was left alone there, the little girl said (conjuring him) :

"You dirty son of your father,

Are you there? Are you alone not thirsty?

Oh, you dirty child of your father!

Dirty child of your father!"

"I am indeed thirsty," said "One-eye," and went away.

Then the two girls came out of the hole, and the younger one took her elder sister on her back, and walked on. As they were going over the bare, tree-less plain, the men saw them, and said, "There they are, far off," and ran after them.

When they came near, the two girls turned themselves into thorn trees, called "Wait-a-bit," and the beads which they wore became gum on the trees. The men then ate of the gum and fell asleep. Whilst they slept, the girls smeared gum over the men's eyes and went away, leaving them lying in the sun.

The girls were already near their kraal, when "One-eye" awoke, and said:

"Oh, the disgrace! fie on thee!

Our eyes are smeared over; fie on thee, my brother!"

Then they removed the gum from their eyes, and hunted after the girls; but the latter reached home in safety, and told their parents what had happened.

Then all lamented greatly, but they remained quietly at home, and did not search for the other girls.

## 42. THE UNREASONABLE CHILD TO WHOM THE DOG GAVE ITS DESERTS;

### OR, A RECEIPT FOR PUTTING ANY ONE TO SLEEP.

(The original, in the o Tyi-hereró or Dámara language, is in Sir G. Grey's Library, J. Rath's Manuscript, pp. 39, 43.)

THERE was a little girl who had an *eïngi* (pronounced *a-inghi*, some kind of fruit). She said to her Mother, "Mother, why is it that you do not say, 'My first-born, give me the *eïngi*?' Do I refuse it?"

"Her Mother said, "My first-born, give me the *eïngi*." She gave it to her and went away, and her Mother ate the *eïngi*.

When the child came back, she said, "Mother, give me my *eïngi*?" but her Mother answered, "I have eaten the *eïngi*!"

The child said, "Mother, how is it that you have eaten my *eïngi*, which I plucked from our tree?" The Mother then (to appease her) gave her a needle.

The little girl went away and found her Father sewing thongs with thorns; so she said, "Father, how is it that you sew with thorns? Why do not you say,

' My first-born, give me your needle ?' Do I refuse ?"
So her Father said, "My first-born, give me your
needle." She gave it to him and went away for a
while. Her Father commenced sewing, but the needle
broke ; when, therefore, the child came back and said,
"Father, give me my needle," he answered, "The
needle is broken ;" but she complained about it, saying, "Father, how is it that you break my needle,
which I got from Mother, who ate my *eïngi*, which I
had plucked from our tree ?" Her Father then gave
her an axe.

Going farther on she met the lads who were in
charge of the cattle. They were busy taking out
honey, and in order to get at it they were obliged to
cut down the trees with stones. She addressed them:
"Our sons, how is it that you use stones in order
to get at the honey ? Why do not you say, 'Our
first-born, give us the axe ?' Do I refuse, or what do
I ?" They said, "Our first-born, give us the axe."
So she gave it them, and went away for some time.
The axe broke entirely. When she came back she
asked, "Where is the axe ? Please give it me." They
answered, "The axe is broken." She then said,
"How is it that you break my axe, which I had received from Father who had broken my needle, which
I got from Mother who had eaten my *eïngi*, which I

had plucked from our tree?" But they gave her some honey (to comfort her).

She went her way again, and met a little old woman, eating insects, to whom she said, "Little old woman, how is it that you eat insects? Why don't you say, ' My first-born, give me honey?' Do I refuse or not?" Then the little old woman asked, "My first-born, give me honey." She gave it her and went away; but presently returning, said, " Little old woman, let me have my honey!" Now the old woman had managed to eat it all during her absence, so she answered, " Oh! I have eaten the honey!" So the child complained, saying, "How is it that you eat my honey, which I received from the lads of our cattle, from our children who had broken my axe, which had been given me by Father who had broken my needle, which was a present from my Mother who had eaten up my *eïngi*, that I had plucked from our tree?"

The little old woman gave her food, and she went away. This time she came to the pheasants, who scratched the ground; and she said, " Pheasants! how is it that you scratch the ground? Why do not you say, ' First-born, give us food?' Do I refuse, or what do I?" They said, "First-born, give." So she gave to them, and went away. When she came back and demanded her food again, they said, " We have eaten the food." She asked, "How is it that you eat my food, which I had received from a little old woman who had eaten up my honey, that I had got from the lads of our cattle who had broken my axe, which had been given me by my Father who had broken my needle, which was a present from my Mother who had eaten my *eïngi,* which I had plucked from our tree?" The pheasants, flying up, pulled out each one a feather and threw them down to the little girl.

She then, walking along, met the children who watched the sheep. They were plucking out hairs from the sheep-skins. So she asked them, "How is it that you pull at these skins? Why do not you say, 'First-born, give us the feathers?' Do I refuse, or what do I?" They said, "First-born, give us the feathers." She gave them and went away, but all the feathers broke. When she returned and said, "Give me my feathers," they answered, "The feathers are broken." Then she complained, "Do you break my feathers which I received from the pheasants who had eaten my food, which had been given me by a little old woman?" They gave her some milk.

She went again on her way, and found their own

handsome dog gnawing bones. She said, "Our dog, how is it that you gnaw these bones?" The dog answered, "Give me milk." She gave it him, and he drank it all. Then she said to the dog, "Give me back my milk." He said, "I drank it." She then repeated the same words which she had spoken so often before ; but the dog ran away, and when she pursued him, he scampered up a tree. She climbed up after him, but the dog jumped down again on the other side. She wanted to do the same, but could not. Then she said, "Our dog, please help me down." He answered, "Why did you pursue me?" and ran away leaving her up the tree.

"That is enough," say the Damara.

# LINGUISTIC PUBLICATIONS

OF

## TRÜBNER & Co.,

60, PATERNOSTER ROW, LONDON, E.C.

.

### MAORI MEMENTOS:

Being a Series of Addresses presented by the Native People
to His Excellency SIR GEORGE GREY, K:C.B., F.R.S.
With Introductory Remarks and Explanatory Notes; to
which is added a small Collection of Laments, &c.

BY CH. OLIVER B. DAVIS.

8vo., pp. iv. and 228, cloth.   Price 12s.

### HANDBOOK OF AFRICAN, AUSTRALIAN, AND POLYNESIAN PHILOLOGY,

As represented in the Library of His Excellency SIR GEO.
GREY, K.C.B., Her Majesty's High Commissioner of the
Cape Colony.   Classed, Annotated, and Edited by

SIR GEORGE GREY AND DR. H. I. BLEEK. ·

Vol.  I.  Part 1.—South Africa, 8vo., pp. 186.  7s. 6d.
Vol.  I.  Part 2.—Africa (North of the Tropic of Capricorn), 8vo., pp. 70.  2s.
Vol.  I.  Part 3.—Madagascar, 8vo., pp. 24.  1s.
Vol.  II.  Part 1.—Australia, 8vo., pp. iv. and 44.  1s. 6d.
Vol.  II.  Part 2.—Papuan Languages of the Loyalty Islands and New Heb-
rides, comprising those of the Islands of Nengone, Lifu,
Aneitum, Tana, and others, 8vo., pp. 12.  6d.
Vol.  II.  Part 3.—Fiji Islands and Rotuma (with Supplement to Part II.,
Papuan Languages, and Part I., Australia), 8vo., pp.
34.  1s.
Vol.  II.  Part 4.—New Zealand, the Chatham Islands, and Auckland Islands,
8vo., pp. 76.  3s. 6d.
Vol.  II.  Part 4 (continuation).—Polynesia and Borneo, 8vo., pp. 77—154. 3s. 6d.
Vol. III.  Part 1.  Manuscripts and Incunables, 8vo., pp. viii. and 24.  2s.

# A COMPARATIVE GRAMMAR OF SOUTH AFRICAN LANGUAGES.

### By DR. W. H. I. BLEEK.

Will be completed in Four Parts. Part I., pp. 104, sewed. 5s.

# THE ISIZULU: A GRAMMAR OF THE ZULU LANGUAGE;

Accompanied with a Historical Introduction, also with an Appendix.

### By REV. LEWIS GROUT.

8vo., pp. liii. and 432, cloth. 21s.

# KAFIR ESSAYS,

And other Pieces; with an English Translation. Edited by

THE RIGHT REV. THE BISHOP OF GRAHAMSTOWN.

32mo., pp. 84, sewed. 2s. 6d.

# A GRAMMAR AND VOCABULARY OF THE NAMAQUA-HOTTENTOT LANGUAGE.

### By HENRY TINDALL, WESLEYAN MISSIONARY.

8vo., pp. 124, sewed. 6s.

# FIRST LESSONS IN THE MAORI LANGUAGE,

### WITH A SHORT VOCABULARY.

### By W. L. WILLIAMS, B.A.

Square 8vo., pp. 80, cloth. London, 1862. 3s. 6d.

www.ingramcontent.com/pod-product-compliance
Lightning Source LLC
Chambersburg PA
CBHW030618270326
41927CB00007B/1229